I0428092

95-1175 ENR

CRS Report for Congress

Humane Treatment of Farm Animals: Overview and Selected Issues

Geoffrey S. Becker
Specialist
Environment and Natural Resources Policy Division

December 6, 1995

CRS

Congressional Research Service · The Library of Congress

Humane Treatment of Farm Animals:
Overview and Selected Issues

SUMMARY

Animal protection activists in the United States are seeking modifications (or even curtailment) of many practices long considered acceptable and necessary to animal agriculture. Examples include rearing large numbers of livestock and poultry in close confinement; performing surgery such as tail-docking or beak-trimming; housing layer hens in cages; and isolating veal calves in crates.

Currently, no Federal law prescribes standards for on-farm handling and care of animals, although two statutes do address the humane transport and slaughter of livestock. All States have anti-cruelty laws, which can--but do not always--cover farm animals. Many States regulate the transport and slaughter of farm animals, but few if any address on-farm activities.

Recent surveys suggest that most people (and many animal protection groups) still support agricultural uses of animals -- but many also appear to support at least some Government regulation to insure humane treatment.

Producers maintain that they understand their animals' welfare needs and address them. They express concern that efforts by poorly informed critics could lead to the imposition of mandatory regulations harmful to producers and animals alike. Support for science, education, and voluntary guidelines are more effective ways of assuring animal welfare, they believe.

But many animal protection groups contend that producer efforts fall short, in part because today's intensive farming systems perpetuate standard practices that are harmful to animals' well-being. More controversial animal "rights" groups believe man has no right to use animals for any purpose.

Conventional agricultural interests have always deployed strong scientific and economic arguments in defense of their industry. However, the 98 percent of the population no longer residing on farms holds an extremely wide range of moral and religious beliefs about man's relationship with other animals--which ultimately could carry more weight in future policy decisions than traditional economic and scientific arguments.

CONTENTS

Humane Treatment of Farm Animals:
Overview and Selected Issues

INTRODUCTION[1]

Animal products are an important part both of the American diet and U.S. agriculture. They contribute about three-quarters of the protein and one-third of the food energy in the U.S. diet. Of the $510 billion that U.S. consumers spent on all domestically produced foods in 1994, nearly half was for meat, poultry, eggs, and dairy products. U.S. farmers and ranchers received $88 billion in 1994 from the sale of animal products, approximately half the value of all agricultural products marketed, according to the U.S. Department of Agriculture (USDA). Crops used for feed brought another $25 billion to $30 billion.[2]

However, the livestock and poultry industries' relationship with the consuming public is changing. Producers today are being asked to respond not only to the traditional market signals of price and quality, but also to newer preferences about *how* food is produced.

One such concern is how animals are treated--an issue viewed by many traditional agricultural interests as the most controversial and, potentially, the most disruptive economically. Animal activists are seeking modifications (or even curtailment) of practices long considered acceptable and necessary to animal agriculture but which they consider inhumane.[3] Examples include rearing large numbers of cattle, hogs, and chickens in close confinement; performing surgical procedures such as castration, tail-docking, or beak-trimming; housing layer hens in cages; and isolating veal calves in crates.

---

[1]The author wishes to thank Janice Swanson, formerly of the U.S. Department of Agriculture's Animal Welfare Information Center and now with Kansas State University, for her valuable assistance.

[2]Stricklin, Wm. Ray, "The Benefits and Costs of Animal Agriculture," from *Science and Animals: Addressing Contemporary Issues*, a conference held by the Scientists Center for Animal Welfare, Washington, D.C., June 22-25, 1988; with updated data from U.S. Department of Agriculture (USDA), Economic Research Service (ERS), various publications.

[3]The terms "animal activist" and "animal protectionist" generally are used here to characterize any group outside of traditional agriculture that would support more aggressive efforts, including but not necessarily limited to Government intervention, to insure the well-being of farm animals. It is not intended to infer that producers and others involved in animal agriculture are not also concerned about animals' well-being.

No Federal law prescribes standards for on-farm handling and care of animals, although two statutes do address the humane transport and slaughter of livestock. Most States have their own anti-cruelty laws, which often--but not always--cover farm animals. A number regulate the transport and slaughter of animals, but virtually none sets rules regarding on-farm activities.

EUROPEAN PRACTICES

By contrast, several European countries have adopted more extensive farm animal treatment regulations.[4] In England, for example, Ruth Harrison's 1964 book *Animal Machines* and a 1965 government report (by the so-called Brambell Committee) eventually led to a series of government actions. These include the creation of a 23-member Farm Animal Welfare Council to advise the Minister of Agriculture, Fisheries, and Food; a 1968 law making it illegal to cause an animal "unnecessary pain or unnecessary distress"; a series of codes of practice for each species enforced by the state veterinary service; and a ban on housing veal calves in crates.

The Swedish parliament in 1988 enacted a law requiring, among other things, that cattle in sheds be able to go outdoors to graze; a 10-year phaseout of so-called "battery cages" for laying hens; an end to tethering sows; standards for bedding for cows and pigs; a humane slaughter mandate; and more authority to regulate genetic engineering and other animal production technologies.

Switzerland has ended the use of battery cages for laying hens, requires bedding and exercise for pigs, regulates veal calves' diets, and sets certain environmental standards for animals. Norway, Denmark, and The Netherlands also have required some changes in animal production methods.

A series of initiatives by the 25-nation Council of Europe and the European Union (EU), have helped to foster these country actions. The Council's March 10, 1976, European Convention for the Protection of Animals Kept for Farming Purposes provided a set of principles on farm animal welfare. EU directives are in force on humane slaughter procedures, size requirements for laying hen cages, and minimum standards for the housing and/or feeding of calves and pigs. Although binding with regard to objective, an EU directive is implemented independently by each member country.

---

[4]Sources include: Baumgartner, Gerhard, "The International (European) Perspective on the Impacts of the Animal Welfare Movement," presented at the Food Animal Well-Being Conference and Workshop in Indianapolis, April 13-15, 1993; Birbeck, Anthony L., "A European Perspective on Farm Animal Welfare," from the April 15, 1991, issue of the *Journal of the American Veterinary Medical Association*; Mason, Jim, and Peter Singer, *Animal Factories*, Harmony Books, New York, 1990; American Farm Bureau Federation (AFBF), *Meeting the Animal Rights Challenge*, 1991; *Agra Europe*, various 1991 issues; and *Animals and Their Legal Rights*, the Animal Welfare Institute, Washington, 1990.

U.S. POLICY SETTING

In the United States, farm animal activism has become a part of the broader, and growing, animal protection movement. Twenty percent of the public has indicated that it has contributed money to animal protection organizations. By one recent count, there are some 7,000, animal protection groups in the United States.[5] Membership in one of the largest, the Humane Society of the United States (HSUS), increased seven times faster between 1984 and 1988 than it had in the preceding 10 years.[6]

These groups and their objectives vary widely.[7] The majority concentrate on local charitable activities--the many local animal shelters and humane societies familiar to most Americans. Others are primarily environmental or wildlife organizations, like the National Wildlife Federation and National Audubon Society.

Several hundred, mostly newer, groups have become highly visible. One controversial national group is People for the Ethical Treatment of Animals (PETA), which advocates an end to all human uses of animals and their products. A few have taken credit for disrupting animal-related work. Other, more established groups, like HSUS, include farm animal care on their broader agendas, but do not necessarily espouse the elimination of animal agriculture.

Several organizations now focus almost exclusively on the treatment of farm animals. These include the Farm Animal Reform Movement (FARM), Farm Sanctuary, the Humane Farming Association, United Poultry Concerns, and the Food Animal Concerns Trust. Some embrace views similar to PETA's, while others espouse--at least publicly--the relatively more modest goal of modifying rather than eliminating animal agriculture.

During the 1980s, the more aggressive groups like PETA had garnered widespread publicity for their efforts to abolish the use of animals in laboratory research. More recently, leading animal activists have predicted that the

---

[5]Mench, Joy A., and Thomas G. Hartsock, "An Update on Animal Welfare Issues"; and Stricklin, W. Ray, and Mench, "Recent Developments in Farm Animal Welfare," from the proceedings of the Maryland Nutrition Conferences of 1992 and 1989, respectively.

[6]HSUS is a national advocacy organization on animal welfare issues supported by dues-paying individuals and is not affiliated with the many local humane societies that operate animal shelters throughout the United States.

[7]Detailed descriptions of these organizations, as well as many farm-related groups, can be found in the *Directory of Animal Rights/Welfare Organizations*, published in 1990 by the Foundation for Biomedical Research, 888 Connecticut Ave., N.W., Ste. 303, Washington, DC 20006.

primary focus of the animal protection movement will shift to farm animals because such animals represent "95 percent of animal suffering."[8]

Farmers, ranchers, animal scientists, agribusiness executives and others in conventional agriculture have always evaluated proposed changes based primarily upon scientific and economic arguments. However, they are now being forced onto unfamiliar debating territory, where considerations other than science and economics could ultimately prevail. Today, the policy setting for animal agriculture issues also includes:

- The production of food for people who are more removed from, and less familiar with, the process than ever before in history; only 2 percent of the U.S. population now resides on farms. Most of the other 98 percent were first introduced to animals on aesthetic or sentimental terms--as pets, zoo subjects, or cartoon characters;

- An extremely wide range of moral and religious beliefs about humans' relationship with other animals, which ultimately could carry more weight than the traditional economic and scientific arguments. Because these beliefs are by their nature arbitrary and value-laden, compromise becomes difficult for many--and impossible for some.

Recent surveys suggest that a majority of the public still supports the use of animals, as do many of the animal protection groups themselves. According to these surveys, and to animal welfare experts, the most widely held views are the following:

- Humans should use animals only when "necessary," currently meaning for food and certain types of biomedical research but perhaps not for cosmetic product testing or furs;

- In general, farmers are treating their animals humanely;

- Animals should not be subjected to needless pain and suffering and, if possible, they should be cared for in ways that enable them to follow their natural behaviors;

- Some level of Government regulation to insure that farm animals are not mistreated might be appropriate.[9]

---

[8]Mongoven, Biscoe, and Duchin Inc., "Decade of the Animals: The Vegetarian Movement," a report on a FARM conference in Rockville, Maryland, on November 8-11, 1991. Also, "Recent Developments in Farm Animal Welfare."

[9]Mench and Hartsock, "An Update on Animal Welfare Issues." Four public opinion surveys on animal agriculture commissioned in 1989 and 1990 by industry groups are summarized in more detail in the AFBF's *Meeting the Animal Rights Challenge*. More recently, an August 1995 telephone survey conducted by Opinion Research Corporation
(continued...)

Agricultural interests themselves have attempted to raise producer awareness of well-being concerns. For example, a number of groups have developed and disseminated their own voluntary guidelines for humane care and treatment of farm animals. The United Egg Producers issued "Recommended Guidelines of Husbandry Practices for Laying Chickens." The National Pork Producers Council has established a committee to address swine care concerns and published its own handbook to guide producers,[10] as has the American Veal Association.

Elsewhere, a consortium of industry groups and Government agencies sponsored the publication in 1988 of an extensive guidebook to assist those engaged in agricultural research and teaching "...in caring for and using agricultural animals in ways judged to be professionally and humanely appropriate."[11] Industry publications frequently feature general and technical articles preaching against mistreatment of animals and explaining improved livestock handling practices.

Luther Tweeten, an agricultural economist and professor at Ohio State University, predicted the course of the debate:

> Animal welfare and rights issues have factual dimensions about which much remains to be learned through research. Ultimately, however, the issues are cultural and political....Reasonable people will look at the same facts, yet reach opposite conclusions for policy because their values and beliefs differ. The success of disparate interest groups in the animal welfare policy decision process will depend on what view of animal welfare wins the hearts and minds of the public.[12]

---

[9](...continued)
for Animal Rights International found that an overwhelming majority agreed that animal pain and suffering should be reduced as much as possible, even though such animals are destined to be slaughtered for food. An overwhelming majority also agreed that Government agencies should be involved, at least to some extent (two-thirds said to a large extent) in protecting farm animals from cruelty.

[10]"Animal Welfare vs. Animal Rights," article in the August-September 1991 issue of *Horizons* magazine, published by Future Farmers of America. Several industry groups are also funding some scientific research on animal well-being; see "Scientific Aspects of Animal Welfare" in this report.

[11]Consortium for Developing a Guide for the Care and Use of Agricultural Animals in Agricultural Research and Teaching, *Guide for the Care and Use of Agricultural Animals in Agricultural Research and Teaching*, March 1988.

[12]Tweeten, Luther, "Public Policy Decisions for Farm Animal Welfare," a paper presented to the International Conference on Farm Animal Welfare, Queenstown, Maryland, June 10, 1991.

ARGUMENTS FOR AND AGAINST ANIMAL AGRICULTURE

Stanley E. Curtis, head of the Department of Dairy and Animal Science at Pennsylvania State University and a nationally recognized authority on farm animal well-being, says the topic is "as complex as a political issue can get."

At one end of a wide spectrum of views are those who hold that man has no right to use animals for *any* purpose, even food or medicine. All animals, these groups contend, have the same inherent right to live a "natural" life as people, and any distinction is "speciesism" and immoral. The modern animal rights movement can trace its roots at least to the mid 1970s, when philosopher Peter Singer published a book called *Animal Liberation*. "The strength of the case for Animal Liberation is its ethical commitment; we occupy the high moral ground and to abandon it is to play into the hands of those who oppose us," the Preface of the book's 1990 edition states.[18]

Supporters of this and similar perspectives shun even a seemingly neutral term such as "animal welfare," which, they believe, implies that man ought to have some dominion over animals; confining them, they say, is cruel by definition. The strictest interpretation of the animal rights view would mean an end to all animal agriculture; ultimately, it leaves no room for compromise with those who make their living in the livestock and poultry industries.

A sharply contrasting view, the product of centuries of Western religious and philosophical thinking, is that God assigned humans a higher place in the world than other animals. Man was given both dominion and stewardship over other forms of life.[14] Carried further, the argument might imply that man is free to exploit animals, and the environment, for his own benefit. Those who believe that animals have the same intrinsic "rights" as man are engaging in anthropomorphism, or the "humanizing" of animals, according to this view. Nonetheless, few if any current adherents to this viewpoint would condone neglect or willful cruelty to animals.

The animal protection movement's strongest critics contend that groups like PETA and FARM illustrate the potential threat that livestock and poultry production faces in coming years. Animal agriculturalists state that they are just as concerned about--and best understand--the welfare needs of their animals and, at any rate, would be economically foolish to mishandle them. They, along with many others in agriculture, are concerned that efforts by a poorly informed public could lead to the imposition of mandatory and unworkable regulations harmful not only to the industry but also to the animals themselves.

---

[18]Singer, Peter, *Animal Liberation*, Random House, New York, 1990.

[14]Stricklin and Mench, "Bioethics and the Professional Animal Scientist," article published in *The Professional Animal Scientist*, June 1989. In the book *The Covenant of the Wild: Why Animals Chose Domestication* (W. Morrow, New York, 1992), Stephen Budiansky argues that domestication evolved naturally, with certain animals essentially yielding their freedom to man in exchange for comfort and security.

However, much of the recent policy debate now focuses on a search for some common consensus on how to ensure farm animal *welfare*. In other words, assuming that man will continue to use animals for food and other necessities, what are the most appropriate methods for taking care of them?[15]

On-Farm Practices at Issue

Many animal protection groups contend that producer efforts will always fall short, in part because today's so-called "factory farming systems" perpetuate standard practices harmful to animals. Following are examples of specific production practices that have come under attack. Many are associated with intensive farming systems.[16]

- **Intensive confinement facilities.** Animal activists charge that confinement systems--including but not limited to large dairy and beef cattle feedlots, and closed chicken houses--can cause both physical suffering and behavioral stress through overcrowded conditions that can foster aggressiveness, cannibalism, boredom, fear, and the spread of diseases (like *Salmonella enteritidis* in poultry houses). They contend that closely confining large numbers of animals makes it extremely difficult to detect individual (often subtle) behavioral changes that might signal serious illness, or to treat them adequately. Activists also argue that animals should be provided enough space to perform their natural behaviors, given access to the out-of-doors for daylight and fresh air, and not be forced to live on concrete or metal-slab or slat floors that can damage legs and feet.

  Defenders of animal agriculture counter that housing systems shelter animals from predators, bad weather, and extreme climates, make breeding and birth less stressful, and in fact do make it easier for farmers to observe and treat each animal, mitigating health and disease problems--which are no more likely to occur in such housing than in the open, they assert. Modern confinement systems, which are continually undergoing improvements based upon new scientific findings, are well-ventilated, warm, sanitary, and facilitate the provision of optimal nutrition and adequate water, they argue.[17]

---

[15]Stricklin and Mench, "Bioethics and the Professional Animal Scientist."

[16]Sources include: Ernst, Stan, "Who's Right," from the March 1990 issue of *Ohio 21*; the American Veterinary Medical Association (AVMA), "Animal Welfare Position Statements and Background Information," revised July 1991; the Council for Agricultural Science and Technology (CAST) report "Scientific Aspects of the Welfare of Food Animals," November 1981; Fox, Michael W., *Farm Animals: Husbandry, Behavior, and Veterinary Practice*, University Park Press, Baltimore, 1984; Mason and Singer, *Animal Factories*.

[17]Animal Industry Foundation, "Animal Myths and Facts," April 1989.

- **Veal crates**. Many activists characterize the raising of veal calves as the least justifiable animal production practice. They contend that the calves are abused physically and psychologically by confining them in separate stalls or crates that are dark and lack room to turn around, providing inadequate nutrition to maintain a light meat color, and dosing them with antibiotics.

  Producers say that modern stall systems do permit calves to stand, lie down, see, touch and react to other calves in clean, well-lit barns. Segregating the calves permits closer medical supervision and controls deadly bacterial diseases and parasites, and diets are specially formulated to meet nutrition and health needs. Group housing for veal calves is inappropriate, because it increases the likelihood of the spread of infectious diseases, according to an AVMA official.[18]

- **Sow gestation stalls**. Activists have criticized the use of gestation stalls for sows which do not permit them to walk or turn around, causing lameness and other problems. Animal scientists and others counter that such systems permit the sow to stand and lie down, reduce death and injury to piglets due to crushing, better control feeding, and reduce aggression, among other benefits.

- **Egg-laying hens**. Activists complain that layers are crowded three, four, or five-abreast into "battery cages" leaving inadequate space to move around, scratch, and eat, and encouraging cannibalism, stress, osteoporosis, and joint diseases. Defenders argue that such housing has protected hens from predators, disease, and weather extremes; fostered better hygiene, environmental control and livability; greatly improved feed conversion and egg production per hen; and helped determine pecking order in small flocks.

- **Beak trimming**. Poultry producers frequently trim the beaks of young chickens and turkeys, often by applying an electrically heated blade, in order to keep chickens from cannibalizing one another. Activists contend that "debeaking" is painful, prevents birds from naturally scratching for food, and that cannibalism is an unwanted consequence of overcrowding.

- **Castration, tail docking, and dehorning**. Routine surgical procedures such as castration of bulls and boars, tail docking of swine, and dehorning of cattle have been criticized as painful and unnecessary, particularly if performed on older animals or without adequate anesthesia. Producers say such procedures are necessary to reduce animal aggressiveness, prevent physical danger to other animals in the herd and to handlers, enhance reproductive control, and/or to satisfy consumer preferences regarding taste and odor of meat. These

---

[18]According to the AVMA, male dairy calves were killed at birth until establishment of the veal industry. About 40 percent of newborn dairy bulls are now raised for veal.

practices are performed on animals at a young age, and do trade "... some short-term discomfort for the long-term benefit of the animals," according to the National Cattlemen's Association (NCA).[19]

- **Use of drugs and chemicals**. Activists argue that confinement housing systems have contributed to an overreliance on antibiotics like penicillin and tetracylines to manage disease and growth, hormones to enhance production and reproduction, and chemicals to control flies, rodents and other pests. Many of these substances--some legal and some not--are dangerous to the health of the animals and producers, it is argued. And, improperly used, they can later show up in the human food supply, posing health hazards such as carcinogenic toxicity, antibiotic resistance, allergic reactions, etc., activists have argued.

  Animal scientists concur that high-density production systems can escalate the potential for diseases. But they also provide a better opportunity than open field systems for closer monitoring of animals' health and nutrition, they state, adding that well-run immunization, nutritional, and environmental systems have greatly curtailed the spread of illnesses. Outbreaks that do occur can be effectively controlled through proper use of scientifically developed drugs proven to pose no threat to human health, defenders say. Growth-promoting antibiotics also have undergone the same level of rigorous development and testing; all animal health products and pesticides are strictly regulated and monitored by the Government to minimize risks to both animals and humans, they maintain.

Related Animal Agriculture Issues

A recent strategy of U.S. animal protection activists has been to reframe the debate within a broader policy context. They see links between animal welfare problems and other perceived ills in production agriculture such as an overdependence on chemical pesticides and fertilizers, environmental pollution, the decline of the family farm and rural areas, and unhealthful food products. By successfully marrying these issues, they also might tap a much broader political constituency.

For example, HSUS and allied organizations have focused on the concept of "humane sustainable agriculture (HSA)," which by one definition "... produces adequate amounts of safe, wholesome food in a manner that is ecologically sound, economically viable, equitable, and humane. HSA meets the animals' basic physical and behavioral requirements for health and well-being through

---

[19]NCA, "Industry Facts: Animal Care," Undated fact sheet.

a food and agricultural system that respects all of nature--humans, soil, water, plants and wild as well as domestic animals."[20]

Economic and Social Issues

Critics frequently note that animal production has been transformed from the smaller, "family-sized" farms of 50 years ago into larger, more intensive operations, where large numbers of animals are confined to closed housing systems to be raised for market as cheaply and rapidly as possible. This has contributed directly to undesirable changes in the structure of U.S. agriculture, they maintain.

"A handful of multinational corporations has now gained a monopolistic control over animal agriculture, with increasing numbers of farmers being either forced out of business or co-opted as contract peons to operate their factory farms or to grow animal feed. Independent farmers are as much a victim of the economy and political pressures of factory farming as are the farm animals themselves," HSUS's Michael Fox has declared.[21]   The decline of small farms has also caused painful dislocations in rural communities, others have argued.

A few in mainstream agriculture say they concur with Fox's view. In the January 1989 issue of *Farm Journal*, Gene Logsdon, a former editor of the magazine wrote: "Which is more a threat to your independent business as a family livestock farmer: animal rights or animal megafactories?.... If large-scale animal factories continue to have their way, you will be slowly pushed out of the hog and beef business just as has happened to 95 percent of the chicken farmers. On the other hand, if the animal rightists have their way, the livestock industry will return to smaller, family-sized farms."

Defenders of animal agriculture acknowledge that farms in general have become larger and more concentrated, and that animal production systems have changed to adjust to increasingly competitive markets. But they point out that most of the Nation's 2 million farms are owned by an individual or married couple responsible for their operation.

On the other hand, USDA considers over 70 percent of U.S. farms to be noncommercial, meaning they produce relatively small quantities of farm products and do not provide enough farm income to support a family. Larger commercial farms--those with annual sales over $250,000 each--accounted for about 5 to 6 percent of all farms, but 57 percent of all agricultural (crop plus livestock) sales. The very largest farms--those with annual sales over $500,000

---

[20]Statement, the Humane Sustainable Agriculture Project, International Alliance for Sustainable Agriculture, Winter 1990-91. A report on this topic is: Benbrook, Charles M., *Sustainable Agriculture in the 21st Century: Will the Grass Be Greener?"* published in collaboration with HSUS, 1991.

[21]"The American Farm and Humane Sustainable Agriculture," speech at the Brookings Institution Agriculture Roundtable, Washington, D.C., February 11, 1992.

each--accounted for about 2 to 3 percent of all farms, but 42 percent of all livestock sales and 38 percent of all agricultural (crop plus livestock) sales.[22]

"Rising labor and land prices have placed a premium on labor-saving and land-saving methods of production. Gains in income and population along with changes in production technologies, including disease control, have interacted with prices to create economies of size and make confinement systems feasible. Small may be beautiful but it is frequently not competitive," a leading agricultural economist has observed.[23]

Penn State's Curtis had noted in 1985: "And lest anyone worry that bigness equals inhumaneness, rest assured (a) that the cruel streak is no respecter of size of operation and (b) that individual inspection of animals is easier in intensive production systems than in extensive ones."[24]

Many farm groups are concerned that the imposition of more government standards for the care and handling of animals will be costly to the industry, and will drive many smaller, financially struggling producers out of business. Besides, it has been argued, consumers have the principal stake in the debate over farm animal welfare. Improvements in productivity on the farm have brought them a wide choice of meat and poultry (and many other) products at reasonable prices. If animal protection advocates are successful in forcing changes--through legislation or other means--that make it more expensive to raise animals, the higher costs will eventually be passed onto consumers (including the poorest families).

Fox and others have countered that welfare-driven changes in animal husbandry could actually save producers money by reducing economic losses caused by stress-related diseases and deaths. Logsdon asserted that even if production costs were higher, many consumers would be willing to pay a few dollars more for their meat and eggs raised the way "the moderate majority of animal rightists desire," just as they may already opt to buy food that is obviously of better quality, or certified as drug or chemical-free.[25]

---

[22]USDA, ERS, *Economic Indicators of the Farm Sector: National Financial Summary, 1993.*

[23]Tweeten, "Public Policy Decisions for Farm Animal Welfare."

[24]"Farm Animal Welfarism in America Today," from the proceedings of the March 21 & 22, 1985, Maryland Nutrition Conference for Feed Manufacturers.

[25]*Farm Journal*, January 1989. According to USDA, the farm value (what farmers receive) of the retail price (what consumers pay) of animal products ranged from 34 percent for cheddar cheese to 56 percent for choice beef and 58 percent for Grade A large eggs in 1993.

Environmental and Resource Issues

Critics maintain that in some parts of the world animal agriculture has contributed to desertification, excessive soil erosion, destruction of wildlife habitat and species, and related problems through overgrazing and destruction of rain forests to make room for rangelands and feed grain cropping. Intensive animal production systems in particular have polluted stream and ground water, concentrating wastes and making it less efficient to return these wastes to crop lands, many argue.[26] Some also have argued that land devoted to the production of expensive protein for wealthy consumers could be put to more constructive use growing crops for the world's hungry and malnourished populations.

Animal agriculturalists agree that inappropriate practices can and have damaged the environment, but that the misuse of animal agriculture in some parts of the world is not a sound argument for its elimination. In fact, "...the appropriate use of farm animals allows more complete recycling of nutrition and conservation of resources within the total ecosystem." Much of the Earth's land is not suitable for food crop production but often can support animals, which in turn can be converted to food for humans, fertilizers, and even fuel.[27] Moreover, most experts primarily attribute world hunger problems not to a shortage of cropland or the diversion of grain to animals, but rather to low incomes, inadequate or inequitable distribution systems (e.g. poor transportation and marketing), civil wars, and other factors not related to production.[28]

Biotechnology Issues

Scientists are now beginning to develop biotechnologies such as embryo transfer, gene insertions, growth hormones, and other laboratory techniques to obtain more desirable productive traits in farm animals. The first product to become commercially available was bovine growth hormone (bovine somatotropin, or BST), approved by the Food and Drug Administration (FDA) in 1994. As of late 1995, an estimated 11 percent of U.S. dairy farms (milking 30 percent of U.S. cows) had adopted BST, which is designed to substantially increase a cow's milk production without a corresponding increase in feed. Another product, porcine somatotropin (PST), which fosters faster growth and leaner meat in hogs, is still in the developmental stages.

---

[26]See for example Durning, Alan B., and Holly B. Brough, *Taking Stock: Animal Farming and the Environment*, Worldwatch Paper 103, July 1991.

[27]Stricklin, "The Benefits and Costs of Animal Agriculture." According to the NCA, at least 80-85 percent of the nutrients consumed by cattle come from sources other than grains, such as grass, roughage, and food processing byproducts.

[28]See for example "Disasters galore: More often than not made, or made worse, by man," from *The Economist*, May 11, 1991.

Animal protectionists have united with other critics who contend that new biotechnologies like BST and PST, along with other modern breeding practices, trade higher productive characteristics for reproductive problems, higher incidence of some diseases, and additional physical and behavioral abnormalities in animals. It has also been argued that such technologies have not been proven completely safe for humans, and that they will accelerate the trend of American agriculture toward a more centralized, vertically integrated structure. Both HSUS and the Humane Farming Association have argued, for example, that cows producing more milk are increasingly prone to mastitis (an udder infection), suffer reproductive problems, have weakened immune systems, and are more susceptible to other diseases which may require the use of more antibiotics and other potentially dangerous drugs.[29]

Supporters contend that biotechnological advances will offer consumers more plentiful food supplies at much lower cost. Some of the emerging technologies will improve nutrition, too, like PST's promise of much leaner cuts of meat, they contend. These advances will make U.S. producers much more efficient and enable them to successfully compete and sell in world markets, supporters argue, maintaining that critics' concerns about animal and human health have no scientific basis. In fact, when FDA approved BST, it concluded that use of the substance poses no health risks to humans. USDA has reported that it is "size neutral," or as readily available to smaller as to larger operations. Similar findings are emerging from scientific and economic studies of PST, supporters note.[30]

Human Nutrition Issues

A number of recent reports by nutrition and health experts have indicated that lower-fat, higher-fiber diets than those presently consumed by most Americans could help lower the risk of certain cancers. A reduction in fat and cholesterol intake has also been recommended to lower the risk of coronary heart disease. In 1988 and 1989, three important reports--*Designing Foods* by the National Academy of Sciences-National Research Council (NAS-NRC) Board on Agriculture, *Diet and Health* by the NAS-NRC Food and Nutrition Board, and the U.S. *Surgeon General's Report on Nutrition and Health*--agreed that the need to reduce fat consumption (to 30 percent of total calories, according to the NAS-NRC) should be the primary priority in public health efforts to prevent

---

[29]Humane Farming Association, "Bovine Growth Hormone." Special Report, 1991. Also, HSUS, "Bovine Somatotropin Statement," December 4, 1990.

[30]For more detailed discussions see: Chite, Ralph, *Bovine Somatotropin (BST or BGH): Questions and Answers on a New Dairy Technology* (CRS Rept. No. 93-1041 ENR), December 13, 1993; and Epstein, Susan, and Irene Stith-Coleman, *Pork Growth Hormone: Agricultural and Regulatory Issues* (CRS Rept. No. 89-661 ENR), December 8, 1989.

chronic disease.[31] Choosing a diet low in fat, saturated fat, and cholesterol is one of the seven key *Dietary Guidelines* jointly issued in 1990 by the Secretaries of Agriculture and Health and Human Services.

Animal protection activists have joined nutrition experts in pointing out that the products of animal agriculture are major sources of fat, saturated fat, and cholesterol in the modern diet. It has even been argued that meat, milk, and eggs have directly contributed to cancer and coronary heart disease.[32] The elimination of meat and poultry from the diet would improve the welfare of humans and farm animals alike, these activists have asserted.

However, many of the same scientists who urge a reduction in fat intake also have recognized the importance of animal products in human nutrition, noting that they can complement the nutritional deficiencies of plant products. Besides contributing about three-quarters of the protein and one-third of the food energy in the American diet, animal products are an easily-obtainable source of vitamin B-12, and are major sources of numerous other vitamins and minerals, particularly iron, calcium, and phosphorus. Although some persons can and do live healthily on completely animal-free diets, they require careful attention to assure adequate intakes of essential nutrients.[33]

In addition, the Surgeon General's recommendations did suggest eating less fat--but not necessarily less meat.[34] Many nutritionists, animal scientists and others agree on the need to cut the consumption of fat consumed through animal products, but they suggest that this can be accomplished through a combination of personal dietary modifications (e.g., shifting from whole to low-fat or skim milk and to leaner cuts of meat) and changes in animal production practices (e.g., alterations of genetic traits and feeding that yield leaner carcasses).[35]

---

[31]Nestle, Marion, and Donna V. Porter, "Evolution of Federal Dietary Guidance Policy: From Food Adequacy to Chronic Disease Prevention," in *Caduceus*, a museum journal for the health sciences, Summer 1990.

[32]See for example Mason and Singer, *Animal Factories*.

[33]Stricklin, "The Benefits and Costs of Animal Agriculture." The American Dietetic Association's official position on vegetarian diets states that "vegetarian diets are healthful and nutritionally adequate when appropriately planned." For background see the *Journal of the American Dietetic Association*, Vol. 88, No. 3, March 1988.

[34]In fact, between 1970 and 1993, animal fat intake decreased by about 28 percent, while vegetable fat increased by 43 percent. USDA, ERS, *Food Consumption, Prices, and Expenditures, 1970-93*, December 1994.

[35]"The Benefits and Costs of Animal Agriculture."

Off-farm Handling Practices

Animal protection groups have also been critical of how farm animals are treated after they leave the farm--during transportation, in sale barns and stockyards, and at slaughterhouses. Among recent questions that have gained relatively wide attention: the handling by some stockyards of sick or injured animals, including nonambulatory ones ("downers"); and whether many chickens and turkeys suffer unnecessarily during slaughter, in part because they are not subject to the Federal Humane Slaughter Act. These and other off-farm issues are discussed in the part of this report on selected legislation.

SCIENTIFIC ASPECTS

"Today, the major controversy in animal welfare is not its importance, but its definition," animal scientist Gary P. Moberg of the University of California recently observed. Scientists who have attempted to address this question have indicated that "welfare," "well-being," and contrasting terms such as "suffering" and "stress" are imprecise and extremely expansive concepts.

One narrow interpretation of the concept holds that poor welfare exists only when an animal's physiology is disrupted enough to endanger survival or reproductive ability, for example. But some have more expansively defined welfare to include not only the animal's physical needs but also its behavioral needs (which some have characterized as its psychological or mental needs). To what extent, if any, do various species experience emotions usually associated with humans? How do animals perceive pain or fear? Do they experience depression or anxiety or social stress?

Various researchers have suggested a variety of indicators that may be important in measuring an animal's overall welfare.[36]

- **Productivity and reproductivity.** One traditional measure has been an animal's productive performance. Many agriculturalists make the case that those who do not provide adequate food, water, shelter, and medical attention will not receive optimal output from their animals. In other words, healthy, happy animals are better producers of meat, milk, eggs, or offspring; and farmers who mistreat their animals risk losing profits, and ultimately the farm.

- **Disease incidence.** It has been suggested that a diseased animal suffers both physically and mentally. Minimizing the incidence of

---

[36]This discussion is based in part on Curtis' testimony before the House Agriculture Subcommittees on Livestock, Dairy, and Poultry, and Department Operations, Research and Foreign Agriculture, June 6, 1989; and Zimbelman, Robert G., "Animal Well-being: One Scientist's Point of View," presented at the annual meeting of the American Society of Animal Science, Laramie, Wyoming, August 8, 1991.

disease and related health problems has long been a goal of sound animal husbandry.

- **Physical safety**. Management systems that shield domestic animals from wild predators, protect them from harming each other, and shelter them from severe weather or other dangerous physical conditions have all been viewed by farmers and ranchers as favorable to their well-being.

- **Physiology and biochemistry**. Some scientists have attempted to calculate animals' overall well-being through quantitative measurements of chemical and other changes in their bodily functions. Examples include levels of leucocytes, adrenalin, growth hormones or other substances in the bloodstream, heart rate, and body temperature.

- **Ethology (behavior)**. Recent studies have attempted to measure how an animal behaves under different situations. A cow or hog or chicken exhibiting "abnormal" behavior might be stressed or suffering. This indicator, according to some researchers, requires an understanding of how the animal would act either in its "natural" environment or if given a choice (of, for example, what to eat or what type of house to live in). It also implies acceptance that a farm animal has at least some awareness of its condition.

Earlier tests of animal welfare relied primarily on productivity measures, perhaps along with disease incidence and physical safety. However, critics of this approach have argued that a producer might sacrifice the welfare and survival of a number of individual animals to maximize overall profits. At any rate, high productivity might have more to do with genetics and feeding practices than with the animals' humane treatment.[37]

Some scientists, particularly those who accept that animals share at least some of the psychological needs traditionally ascribed to humans, assert that physiological and behavioral measurements are the most direct indicators of animal stress.

A growing consensus among animal scientists and others is that animal well-being can best be assessed through an interdisciplinary approach, one that considers a wide range of indicators rather than any single one. It has been argued that these indicators must be applied "holistically" to each animal's situation: how it is housed and fed, how it relates to others in its species, and so forth.

Animal agriculture, supported by more than a century of Federal research and extension programs, has made enormous strides in the areas of animal productivity, disease prevention, and even physical safety. The introduction of sophisticated genetic selection, nutritionally balanced feeds, new veterinary

---

[37]Fox, *Farm Animals: Husbandry, Behavior, and Veterinary Practice.*

medicines, and new, climate-controlled housing systems have brought major economic benefits to producers and consumers alike. For example, a hen today can lay twice as many eggs as she did 50 years ago, on 50 percent less feed. Broilers are now raised to a slaughter weight of 4.2 pounds in well under 2 months, compared with 3 pounds in 2.5 months in 1955. The average dairy cow now produces three times as much milk as 50 years earlier.

It is no coincidence that science has been able to measure objectively and quantify numerically these traditional indicators of performance--as in rates of growth and production, feed efficiency, and mortality. But the more contentious aspects of animal well-being--those associated with an animal's possible mental state--are much more subjective and difficult to quantify, analyze and interpret, animal scientists and veterinarians generally agree. Some traditional agricultural interests have simply dismissed such efforts, insisting that it is impossible to prove that farm animals either do or do not suffer mentally.

Fox has written that any inability to assess scientifically what an animal (or, for that matter, a human being) experiences subjectively or emotionally is no reason to ignore their importance:

> The close alliance of science and economics in animal production and farm and laboratory animal care does not make such fields the exclusive domain of science and technology, for there is no legitimate or logical reason for excluding ethics, values, and humane concerns on the basis of their being irrelevant or "unscientific." ... In order to avoid "paralysis by analysis" in defining optimal conditions scientifically, common sense morality, empathy, and ethics should be an integral part of the decision-making process in deciding how animals should be husbanded.[38]

Joy A. Mench of the University of Maryland Department of Poultry Science, and Ari van Tienhoven of the Cornell University Department of Poultry and Avian Sciences, observed:

> There is considerable controversy...over whether emotional experiences like boredom, frustration, and apprehension of future suffering or pleasure exist in an evolutionary continuum or are unique to human beings. Nevertheless, devising methods to quantify and interpret the emotional states of animals has become the central problem for ethologists investigating farm animal welfare.[39]

Mench and others assert that science can and should help to answer questions about whether and how animals "feel." Failure to apply scientific criteria to this most-contested area of animal welfare will likely lead to the

---

[38]*Farm Animals: Husbandry, Behavior, and Veterinary Practice.*

[39]Mench, Joy A., and Ari van Tienhoven, "Farm Animal Welfare," in the November-December 1986 issue of *American Scientist.*

adoption of government standards that might be well-intentioned but harmful to the animals they were designed to protect, they add.

At the 1993 conference on food animal well-being, a work group of animal experts identified three general areas for research that, they believe, should receive priority:

- **The adaptation and adaptiveness of farm animals to their environment;** to determine (and quantitatively measure) individual animals' ability to adapt, physiologically and behaviorally, to today's intensive production methods, given each's genetic (inherited) constraints;

- **Social behavior and space requirements of domestic animals.** More specifically, a better understanding of food animal social behavior could help determine whether, and how, restricted space affects animal well-being;

- **Cognition and motivation of domestic animals**, to determine and quantify if possible what they sense and perceive emotionally, and to evaluate their motivational states (hunger, comfort, etc.) under various conditions.

Once research in these areas yields improved, science-based measurements of well-being, the appropriate short-term production practices and long-term management systems can be developed. These will assist the livestock industry to address emerging ethical and societal concerns.[40]

Meanwhile, funding for such work appears relatively limited, according to animal science professionals. At USDA, which spends some $200 million or more annually on all research related to animal agriculture, objectives have long focused on increasing productivity, improving product quality and safety, and lowering costs. USDA officials have stated that much of this work has contributed to animal well-being through major improvements in animal health and safety.

Nonetheless, relatively few of these dollars are devoted to research that USDA identifies primarily or specifically as animal welfare-related. Officials at USDA's Agricultural Research Service (ARS), which is responsible for in-house research, identified about $1.8 million in spending for activities related to animal well-being, out of an estimated $109.1 million on all projects involving livestock and poultry, in fiscal year 1995. At the Department's Cooperative State Research, Education, and Extension Service (CREES), which supports research through the State land grant universities, about $2.7 million out of a total

---

[40]Moberg, Gary P., and Mench, "Researchable Problems and Priorities Related to Animal Well-Being," report on a work group that met at the 1993 Conference on Food Animal Well-Being.

animal research budget of $99.2 million was identified as directed toward animal well-being in fiscal year 1993, the most recent year available.[41]

Several producer groups said they also have funded scientific research related to well-being. For example, the Animal Industry Foundation, an organization which promotes producers' views on animal care issues, established a scientific advisory panel and has provided several grants for scientific symposia and research projects. The pork industry has spent several hundred thousand dollars on scientific research into the behavioral and physiological needs of hogs.

Animal scientists and critics alike predict that financing for stress-related research could increase in coming years, particularly if the farm animal well-being issue gains more political visibility. Animal activists question its likely emphasis, which, they contend, will be genetic and pharmaceutical solutions to the so-called animal stress problem. Many animal scientists disagree, predicting that more future work will be aimed at accommodating animals' natural behavioral needs--as evidenced by the discussions at the 1993 conference about adjusting short and long-term production practices in response to scientific findings.

EXISTING FEDERAL AND STATE LAWS

No Federal law prescribes standards for on-farm handling and care of animals. However, two U.S. statutes do set guidelines for humane transport and slaughter.

At the State level, virtually all legislatures have enacted general animal anti-cruelty laws; some cover, and some specifically exempt, agriculture. A number of States regulate the transport and/or slaughter of farm animals, but apparently none set standards for on-farm animal care.[46] Animal welfare groups contend that the current body of law affecting livestock is inadequate; HSUS, for example, has characterized it as "at best, haphazard."[47]

These groups seek to expand legal protections for animals, including farm animals, in two ways: (1) by lobbying national and State lawmakers for new laws, and (2) by challenging both the interpretation and enforcement of existing statutes in judicial proceedings.

---

[41]USDA, *1996 Budget Explanatory Notes for Committee on Appropriations*; also telephone communications with ARS and CSREES budget officials, November 15, 1995. Critics assert that the Department may be overly broad in its definition of well-being, including, for example, research on animal health (disease prevention).

[46]Many counties and municipalities have animal ordinances, including anti-cruelty provisions, but these are not addressed in this report.

[47]Humane Society of the United States. *Livestock Cruelties State Legislative Action Packet*, 1984.

Producers and other agricultural interests, on the other hand, generally support present laws. "The legal changes espoused by (animal) rightists at both the State and Federal levels would broaden the standards for 'humane' treatment of animals to change the way animals are raised, handled, transported and slaughtered."[48]

Recent commentary by Ohio State agricultural economist Tweeten raises a different concern about efforts to change the laws. He argued that any major animal welfare legislation must be Federal "... because any State that raises production costs with substantive animal welfare legislation will be unable to compete in the market with other States."[49]

If so, it can also be argued that animal welfare policy has significant international aspects. Meat and poultry exports have grown markedly in recent decades. U.S. producers' ability to maintain and expand their overseas markets depends not only on both their own and foreign competitors' production costs, but also on the various government standards and regulations that affect these costs. Countries with relatively stringent animal welfare standards are likely to want their foreign competitors to abide by equivalent standards. (The EU directive requiring beef to be produced without growth hormones--although adopted more out of perceived safety rather than animal welfare concerns--is a case in point. The directive has been a major obstacle in Europe for U.S. beef exporters.)

Just how far society might be willing to extend the legal status of farm (and other) animals remains to be seen. Noting that a growing body of literature is arguing for the recognition of legal rights for animals, a 1983 book on animal law observed:

> Since the legal system at present does not allow for any rights to be held by animals, the 'rights' movement has a substantial task ahead of it .... For the foreseeable future any legal advancement will be of the protective nature, as it would require a substantial change of attitude and awareness before the idea of legal rights for animals could be accepted. To obtain such rights, the Constitution of the United States would have to be amended, just as it was necessary to amend the Constitution to give all the human races legal rights.[50]

---

[48]American Farm Bureau Federation. *Meeting the Animal Rights Challenge.*

[49]Promoters of a 1988 voter referendum to impose farm animal care standards in Massachusetts had argued that, on the contrary, such standards would make the State's farmers more competitive among consumers, who are now taking a deeper interest in how their food is produced. See: Japenga, Ann. "Livestock Liberation: A Revolution May Be Brewing as Animal Activists Challenge Conditions Down on the Farm." *Harrowsmith*, November/December 1989.

[50]Favre, David S., and Murray Loring. *Animal Law.* 1983.

Federal Laws[51]

The Twenty-Eight Hour Law, which regulates the movement of livestock by rail and water, and the Humane Slaughter Act are the only major Federal statutes affecting the handling of farm animals. Several other animal protection laws pertinent to the animal welfare debate are also described below.

Agricultural Animal Research [P.L. 95-113 and P.L. 101-624; 7 U.S.C. 3191-3201 and 5801(a)(5)]

These sections are within Federal statutes guiding the direction of USDA-sponsored agricultural research. Among stated research objectives are to promote "the improved health and productivity of domestic livestock, poultry, aquatic animals, and other income-producing animals which are essential to the Nation's food supply...." The law was amended in 1990 to require the Secretary of Agriculture to commission a National Academy of Sciences study "of the delivery system utilized to provide farmers...and ranchers with animal care and veterinary medical services, including animal drugs." The study is to assess opportunities to, among other things, "advance the well-being and treatment of farm animals."

The Secretary also was directed to establish an Animal Health Science Research Advisory Board to provide advice on animal health and disease research, which shall include a representative of "an organization concerned with the general protection and well-being of animals." Another part of the law authorized funding for "research designed to increase our knowledge concerning agricultural production systems that" serve six specified purposes, one of which is to "promote the well being of animals."

Animal Welfare Act [P.L. 89-544; 7 U.S.C. 2131-2159]

The principal Federal animal protection law excludes farm animals from its coverage, even though it is administered by USDA. The 1966 law was amended and expanded by laws in 1970 (P.L. 91-579), 1976 (P.L. 94-279), 1985 (P.L. 99-198), and 1990 (P.L. 101-624). The statute authorizes the Secretary to "promulgate standards to govern the humane handling, care, treatment, and transportation of animals by dealers, research facilities, and exhibitors." Standards must include requirements "for animal care, treatment, and practices in experimental procedures to ensure that animal pain and distress are minimized...."

The law excludes from the definition of animal "...horses not used for research purposes and other farm animals, such as, but not limited to livestock or poultry, used or intended for use as food or fiber, or livestock or poultry used

---

[51]Unless otherwise noted, this section is from: Cohen, Henry. *Brief Summaries of Federal Animal Protection Statutes* (CRS Rept. No. 94-731 A), revised October 24, 1994; and *Animals and Their Legal Rights*.

or intended for use for improving animal nutrition, breeding, management, or production efficiency, or for improving the quality of food or fiber."

The official legislative history of the Animal Welfare Act does not explain why farm animals have always been excluded. The original intent of the Act was to curb the theft and mistreatment of dogs and cats for experimental and research purposes. The subsequent amendments also indicated that lawmakers' attentions were more directed to specific concerns outside of agriculture, such as the shipping of pets on public transportation, dog fighting, and the use of most warm-blooded animals in biomedical experiments.

Humane Slaughter Act [P.L. 85-765; 7 U.S.C. 1901-1906]

The Humane Slaughter Act is enforced by USDA's Food Safety and Inspection Service (FSIS) under provisions of the Federal Meat Inspection Act [21 U.S.C. 603(b), 610(b), 620(a)]. The law's key provisions are:

No method of slaughter or handling in connection with slaughtering shall be deemed to comply with the public policy of the United States unless it is humane. Either of the following two methods of slaughtering and handling are hereby found to be humane:

(a) in the case of cattle, calves, horses, mules, sheep, swine, and other livestock, all animals are rendered insensible to pain by a single blow or gunshot or an electrical, chemical or other means that is rapid and effective, before being shackled, hoisted, thrown, cast, or cut; or

(b) by slaughtering in accordance with the ritual requirements of the Jewish faith or any other religious faith that prescribes a method of slaughter whereby the animal suffers a loss of consciousness by anemia of the brain caused by the simultaneous and instantaneous severance of the carotid arteries with a sharp instrument and handling in connection with such slaughtering.

The original 1958 act was sponsored chiefly by Senator Hubert Humphrey and Representative W.R. Poage, then chairman of the House Agriculture Committee. It covered packinghouses that sold meat to the Federal Government, which then accounted for about 80 percent of the industry. In 1978, legislation sponsored by Senator Robert Dole and Representative George Brown, Jr. effectively extended coverage to virtually all U.S. plants that slaughter red meat animals for human consumption, and to imports.

Chickens, turkeys, and other birds currently are not subject to humane slaughter requirements. Proposed legislation to include poultry has been introduced into the 102nd, 103rd, and 104th Congresses.

Twenty-Eight Hour Law [Act of June 29, 1906; 45 U.S.C. 71-74]

The law was first enacted in 1873 in response to intense criticism of cattle transportation methods. At the time, animals were routinely shipped over long distances in overcrowded steamships and railcars without food or water. Many would arrive at stockyards emaciated, injured, or dead. In 1906, a stronger Twenty-Eight Hour Law replaced the earlier version and remains in effect.

The measure, also known as the "Cruelty to Animals Act, " the Live Stock Transportation Act," and the "Food and Rest Law," regulates the transport of animals across State lines by rail or water, but not by motor vehicle or aircraft, which were not in general use in 1906. Today, most livestock shipments are by truck--thus, few animals are effectively covered at the Federal level (also see State Laws, below). Amendments to extend coverage to motor vehicles have not been successful, USDA's Animal and Plant Health Inspection Service (APHIS), which administers the law, has observed.

The Twenty-Eight Hour Law prohibits the confinement of animals in "[railroad] cars, boats, or vessels of any description for a period longer than twenty-eight consecutive hours without unloading the same in a humane manner, into properly equipped pens, for rest, water, and feeding, for a period of at least five consecutive hours, unless prevented by storm or by other accidental or unavoidable causes ...." Three exceptions are that (1) confinement may be extended to 36 hours upon written request of the owner or custodian; (2) sheep may be confined for up to 36 hours if the 28-hour period expires at night; and (3) animals do not have to be unloaded if they "have proper food, water, space, and opportunity to rest" on board.

State Laws

State legislation affecting animal welfare is generally more extensive than the Federal statutes. But many State laws differ in their coverage of farm animals. Many States, like the Federal Government, have intervened with other laws and regulations to assure fair trading and to prevent the spread of diseases, which are aimed primarily to benefit owners economically rather than animals' welfare *per se*. Certain State environmental and food safety laws may also have at least partial impact on animal well-being.

However, virtually no State has taken an interventionist approach to farm animal well-being. That is, none regulates animal production practices on the farm or ranch itself (although a number do address transportation and slaughter to varying degrees).

The most significant effort in the United States to impose on-farm standards of care occurred in 1988 in Massachusetts. Animal protection activists had placed on the election ballot a referendum on whether to institute regulations "to ensure that farm animals are maintained in good health and that cruel or inhumane practices are not used in the raising, handling or transportation of farm animals." The unsuccessful referendum would have directed the State to regulate animal production practices like the raising of veal calves, dehorning and castration of cattle, and the disposal of male chickens at hatcheries, for example. Led by the Massachusetts Farm Bureau, agricultural interests mounted a campaign arguing that the referendum, known as Question 3, would hurt the State's family farmers. Question 3, once apparently favored by a majority of the voters, eventually was defeated by a 71 to 29 percent margin.[52]

Instead of standards like those proposed for Massachusetts, most States have chosen to enact anti-cruelty statutes imposing various criminal penalties on violators. In general, these statutes make it a crime to torture or cruelly beat an animal, or to deprive it of food and water. In most, farm animals appear to be implicitly included in the general definition of "animal." However, several States specifically exempt accepted animal agricultural practices from coverage. In addition, a profusion of qualifying phrases in legal wording (see below) make it unclear exactly how farm animals might be covered in numerous States.

More specifically, nearly half the States have laws stipulating that cruel treatment must be willful or malicious. Nearly 20 prohibit the deprivation of both "necessary sustenance" and food and water; in several others, only "necessary sustenance" is mentioned. Brief references requiring the provision of adequate space, light, ventilation, and/or clean living conditions are made in the statutes of Florida, Maine, Maryland, Minnesota, North Dakota, New York, Ohio, Washington, and Wisconsin.[53]

The major issues regarding these anti-cruelty statutes are their interpretation and enforcement. As this report has indicated, there is little agreement among agricultural producers and animal protection activists on the meanings of such terms as animal well-being, cruelty and mistreatment. And qualifying phrases like "unnecessarily," "intentionally," "recklessly," and "maliciously" appear frequently in State legislation. Can such qualifiers be interpreted as "a license to inflict any degree of suffering on any number of animals provided that the motives of the person inflicting the pain are not sadistic," as the Animal Welfare Institute has argued?[54] HSUS has declared: "Most anti-cruelty statutes specifically prohibit the very types of activities that occur in the livestock industry."[55]

On the other hand, most producers would likely argue that the existing laws provide adequate protection for animals. AFBF's animal rights handbook observes that "...virtually every person in the business of animals would be hard-

---

[52]*Harrowsmith*, November/December 1989.

[53]*Animals and Their Legal Rights.*

[54]*Ibid.*

[55]"Livestock Cruelties State Legislative Action Packet."

pressed to justify anything less than the highest standards" against animal abuse and neglect. But other questions like "deprivation" are harder to define: "Is a chicken caged in close confinement 'deprived' of space in a manner that undermines its welfare? Do hogs raised under accepted conditions of animal husbandry undergo *un*acceptable stress?" AFBF asked. Noting the lack of a strict scientific basis for determining stress, it added: "...ambiguities in the language (of the State anti-cruelty laws) may pave the way for lawsuits" by activists.[56]

For example, North Dakota defines cruelty as acts or omissions causing "unnecessary or unjustifiable" pain, suffering or death; what then is "unnecessary or unjustifiable"? Other States exempt "normal" animal husbandry practices--but could legal challenges redefine producers' accepted notion of "normal?"

SELECTED LEGISLATION

Over the past 25 years, Congress has enacted a series of laws gradually increasing the regulation of animals, particularly those used in biomedical and related research. Animal protection activists now appear to be shifting more of their attention to the treatment of farm animals. However, their efforts have culminated in no significant new legislation at the Federal level since the 1978 amendments to the Humane Slaughter Act of 1958.[57]

Although the current policy debate over farm animal welfare is broadly cast, bills affecting agriculture have been few and focused on specific issues. As of late 1995, none had advanced beyond the committee stage. A brief discussion of selected bills follows.

Downed Animals

Proposal: The Downed Animal Protection Act (H.R. 2143, introduced into the 104th Congress on July 31, 1995, by Representative Ackerman) would amend the Packers and Stockyards Act to make it unlawful for any stockyard owner, market agency, or dealer to market or hold "nonambulatory" livestock unless they have been humanely killed.

---

[56]"Meeting the Animal Rights Challenge."

[57]Although one bill related to farm animal welfare has been enacted in recent years, it is aimed at protecting producers and research facilities from radical activist groups. The Animal Enterprise Protection Act of 1992 (P.L. 102-346; 18 U.S.C. 43) makes it a Federal crime to cause "physical disruption to the functioning of an animal enterprise by intentionally stealing, damaging, or causing the loss of, any property (including animals or records) used by the animal enterprise..." and thereby cause damages exceeding $10,000.

Background: Nonambulatory livestock, commonly called "downers," are animals that are disabled due to illness or injury. At issue is whether these animals are treated inhumanely by haulers, stockyards, and packing houses while they are being held or moved for slaughter. The treatment of downers received widespread public attention in May 1991 after NBC News' *Expose* show featured videotapes of weak, emaciated animals at the South St. Paul stockyards in Minnesota. Similar bills were introduced into the 102nd Congress (S. 2296) and the 103rd Congress (S. 367 and H.R. 559), but did not advance. However, downers were among numerous topics discussed at hearings on USDA's Packers and Stockyards Administration held January 15 and March 5, 1992, and on September 28, 1994, by a subcommittee of the House Agriculture Committee.

Pro: Outlawing the sale or transfer of nonambulatory livestock would encourage producers to take better care of their animals by removing some of the financial incentive for sending them to stockyards for some salvage value; promote greater care during loading and transport; and generally reduce these animals' suffering.

Con: Livestock industry leaders generally agree that livestock markets should not accept severely disabled animals. However, it will always be impossible to insure that no animal will become disabled during transport and marketing. Nevertheless, the vast majority of those in the industry humanely treat their animals; it has been estimated that downers account for less than a tenth of a percent of all animals at stockyards, and few have been accepting them since the 1991 reports, at any rate. Federal legislation is unwarranted, because the industry is already responding aggressively through education and market pressure.

Poultry Slaughter

Proposal: The Humane Methods of Poultry Slaughter Act of 1995 (H.R. 264, introduced into the 104th Congress on January 4, 1995, by Representative Jacobs) would amend the Poultry Products Inspection Act to require the poultry industry to comply with the requirements of the Federal Humane Slaughter Act.

Background: The Humane Slaughter Act of 1958 (P.L. 85-765), as amended by the Humane Methods of Slaughter Act of 1978 (P.L. 95-445), requires all livestock under Federal meat inspection to be slaughtered humanely. Poultry have always been excluded from the requirement, which is enforced by USDA's Food Safety and Inspection Service (FSIS). Currently, meat birds are first hung by their feet and electrically stunned to render them insensible before their arteries are cut with an automatic knife. Representative Jacobs also had introduced these bills into the 102nd Congress (H.R. 4124) and 103rd Congress (H.R. 649). Although H.R. 649 was one of the subjects of the September 1994 hearing before a House Agriculture subcommittee, no other action occurred.

Pro: Many birds are subjected to needless pain and suffering, because current slaughter systems do not always kill or cause meat birds to lose consciousness prior to bleeding, and because laying hens are usually not stunned at all. The bill would end this problem by forcing poultry producers to comply with the same requirements long in place for the red meat industry.

Con: Current slaughter systems are humane and do cause immediate unconsciousness in meat birds. Laying hens cannot be stunned effectively because their bones are too brittle to withstand the electrical shock necessary to render them insensible; broken bones cause meat quality to suffer, resulting in large economic losses for producers. More research needs to be completed on alternative stunning methods (such as gas) before unworkable, costly new requirements are imposed.

Veal Calf Production

Proposal: Legislation (H.R. 263, introduced into the 104th Congress on January 4, 1995, by Representative Jacobs) is intended to protect veal calves by prohibiting certain practices regarding enclosure space and diet. Violators would be subject to specified civil and criminal remedies; inspections by the Secretary of Agriculture or any designated representative would be authorized.

Background: H.R. 263 is similar to legislation introduced in 1988 (H.R. 2859), 1989 (H.R. 84), 1990 (S. 2346), 1991 (H.R.252), and 1993 (H.R. 1455). None of the measures has emerged from committee. However, the House Agriculture Subcommittees on Livestock, Dairy, and Poultry, and on Department Operations, Research, and Foreign Agriculture did hold a joint hearing on H.R. 84 on June 6, 1989.

Pro: Many activists characterize the raising of veal calves as one of the least humane animal production practices. They contend that the calves are abused physically and psychologically by separating them from their mothers, confining them in separate stalls or crates that lack room to turn around, providing inadequate nutrition to obtain a light meat color, and dosing them with antibiotics. H.R. 263 would mandate improvements in animal care that the industry will not undertake voluntarily.

Con: Producers respond that stall systems permit calves to stand, lie down, see, touch and react to other calves in clean, well-lit barns. Segregating the calves permits closer medical supervision and controls deadly bacterial diseases and parasites, and diets are specially formulated to meet diet and health needs. Legislation like H.R. 263 reflects a misunderstanding of modern veal production, is not based upon farmer experience or science, and would be economically devastating to the industry, opponents have argued.

Horse Transportation

Proposal: Legislation (S. 1283, introduced into the 104th Congress on September 28, 1995, by Senator McConnell) is aimed at regulating the welfare of horses while they are being shipped to facilities for slaughter. The "Safe Commercial Transportation of Horses for Slaughter Act of 1995" would, among other things, require that horses be rested off a vehicle and have access to food and water after 24 hours; that vehicles meet safety and comfort standards, and that the horses themselves be physically fit to travel.

Background: This bill is a modified version of legislation (S. 2522) introduced into the 103rd Congress by Senator McConnell. Its introduction had followed an investigation by the Humane Society of the United States (HSUS) into the treatment of horses after they are sold for slaughter.

Pro: Legislation is needed because current laws permit horses destined for slaughter to be transported in overcrowded trailers with inadequate headroom. Horses, unlike other livestock, must be moved over long distances because so few horse slaughter facilities exist in the United States. Moreover, the HSUS investigation found that horses are inadequately watered and fed, may be downers, and mistreated by handlers during transport and at slaughterhouses.

Con: Livestock interests agree that horses should be treated humanely when sold and transported to slaughter. Critics of the bill believe groups such as the HSUS have used anecdotal evidence to condemn an entire industry, most of which already provides adequate care. More Government regulation would be both unnecessary and burdensome for this responsible group. As with the downer problem, aggressive education and market pressure will be far more effective than new legislation to deal with the minority who do abuse such horses.